Li

THE SCHOOL SURVIVAL GUIDE
Written so even you can understand it

Brough Girling

Illustrated by Judy Brown

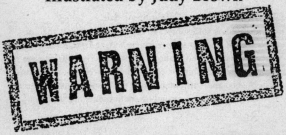

NOT SUITABLE FOR ADULTS

First published in Great Britain in Lions in 1994
Lions is an imprint of HarperCollins Children's Books,
a division of HarperCollins Publishers Ltd, 77-85 Fulham Palace
Road, Hammersmith, London W6 8JB
3 5 7 9 10 8 6 4

ISBN 0 00 674740 X

Printed and bound in Great Britain
by HarperCollins Manufacturing Ltd, Glasgow

Lions
An Imprint of HarperCollins*Publishers*

WARNING

BEWARE. This book is not suitable for adults* or teachers or librarians. It should not be read by people of a delicate disposition or, for instance, children who are afraid of the dark, spiders, ghosts, snakes, or dinner ladies.

Also, if your mum or dad find you reading this book when you should be doing your homework, you'll be in big trouble. **DON'T SAY I DIDN'T WARN YOU.**

SPECIAL SURVIVAL TIP *Conceal this book inside the jacket of an old copy of something cheesy like* The Water Babies *or* Heidi *or* What Katie Did Next. *Adults will be so pleased that you're reading something sensible for a change.*

* After all, there are lots of adult books that are unsuitable for children; this book is like them, only the other way round.

3

AUTHOR'S DEDICATION

The author would like to dedicate this book to school children everywhere – especially those who have coughed up a measly few quid to buy it.

AND DISCLAIMER

THIS BOOK IS A WORK OF NON-FICTION, AND THEREFORE ANY SIMILARITIES BETWEEN THE CHARACTERS IN IT AND ACTUAL PEOPLE, ESPECIALLY TEACHERS, ARE ENTIRELY INTENTIONAL.

WHAT THE CRITICS HAVE SAID ABOUT THIS BOOK

'Cor, what a stonker! A bloomin' brill book and a right rollickin' read – or I'm not the Archbishop of Canterbury.
Not The Archbishop of Canterbury

'It's not as good as any book by Dick King-Smith.'
Dick King-Smith

'Unfortunately it contains nothing at all about the breeding and hand-rearing of edible snails or small slugs...'
The Edible Snail And Small Slug Breeders' Gazette

'The paper may not be recycled, but at least the jokes are.'
Jonathon Porridge

'If this wonderful book had been available when I was a boy I might have made more of a success of my education, and gone on to do a really sensible, worthwhile job.'
The Prime Minister

KNOW YOURSELF AND SURVIVE

If you've ever seen great mountaineers or explorers being interviewed on TV you may have heard them say that having to survive through difficulty or danger helps them to 'know themselves'. Going to school, of course, means having to survive through difficulties and danger, so in the first section of this amazing book we give you a head start by helping you to 'know yourself'.

FILL THIS IN – AND KEEP IT SECRET!
MY NAME IS:
IF I COULD CHOSE ANOTHER FIRST
NAME IT WOULD BE:
MY SCHOOL IS:

Put a circle round any of the following
words that you think describe your school –
BRILL, GHASTLY, GHASTLY, COOL,
CRUEL, CHAOTIC, STINKY, MEGA-
WICKED, ACE, HELLISH, ANTIQUE,
INHUMAN, RADICAL, MEDIEVAL, HIP,
FANDABBYDOSEY, PREHISTORIC,
CRUMMY.

MY FAVOURITE COLOUR IS:
MY FAVOURITE POP GROUP IS:

MY BEST SCHOOL SUBJECT IS:
MY WORST SCHOOL SUBJECT IS:

MY FAVOURITE TEACHER IS:
THEIR NICKNAME IS:
I LIKE THEM BECAUSE:

MY WORST TEACHER IS:
THEIR NICKNAME IS:

Put a circle round any of these words that describe your worst teacher – CHEESY, DECOMPOSING, DIM, DUMB, DAFT, TYRANNICAL, DIABOLICAL, PLAIN, PLAIN STUPID.

HEADTEACHER'S NAME (IF DIFFERENT FROM TEACHERS' ABOVE):

Who is your headteacher most like? Put a circle round appropriate names – INDIANA JONES, POSTMAN PAT, GAZZA, MRS THATCHER, THE ENGLISH RUGBY TEAM, NODDY, FRANKEN-STEIN, GORDON THE GOPHER.

Put a circle round any of the following words which describe what you want to be when you grow up – TRAIN DRIVER, ADULT, EXPLORER, TAX INSPEC-TOR, FILM STAR, TEACHER, PRIME MINISTER, DINNER LADY, FOOT-BALLER, LIKE MY MUM, SPACEMAN.

A USER'S GUIDE TO SCHOOLS

If you're having to try to survive in a school – it's best to know what type of school you actually go to!

There are surprisingly few basic types of school – though many schools combine the horrific characteristics of several of them.

Throughout this School Survival Guide there are sections which examine basic types of school. Here is the first:

PART ONE:
ST BLUE PETER'S SCHOOLS

ST BLUE PETER'S SCHOOLS are quite common – you can come across them any day of the week – especially Mondays and Thursdays.

MAIN CHARACTERISTICS

The most striking main characteristic of these schools is that they are absolutely crawling with pet animals. Large Labrador or Retriever type dogs, tabby cats with loads of kitten – even tortoises, gerbils, hamsters, giraffes, elephants and rhino.

TEACHING METHODS

It's all jolly friendly – and jolly jolly. There is masses of handicraft, nature study, gardening, cookery and, of course, High Adventure. The teachers are inclined to be very young and happy, and they smile a lot. You can always tell a ST BLUE PETER SCHOOL from the way they start their Assemblies:

FOOD
These schools are remarkable in that the pupils are shown how to make their own food. It's nearly always 'something I prepared earlier'.

UNIFORM
There isn't exactly a uniform (clean jeans and bright T-shirts are normal): but special badges are worn, and are absolutely essential.

BAD FOR
Sulky children who couldn't care less

about the environment and want to watch ITV all the time.

GOOD FOR
ST BLUE PETER SCHOOLS are very good for children who like animals and high adventure. Also anyone with a lot of yoghurt pots, egg boxes and wire coat hangers that they don't know what to do with.

SPECIAL COMMENTS
If you go to one of these schools make sure you wear your badge and smile a lot.

HAZARDS OF SCHOOL LIFE

NOTES TO TAKE HOME

NOTES TO TAKE HOME nearly always mean trouble. They always mean that your teachers want to tell your parents something – i.e. BAD NEWS. For instance:

TAKE A NOTE HOME: SURVIVAL TIPS

It's not always possible to counteract completely the effects of having to take a note home – but some survival tips can be used to limit the damage caused by this particular teacher guerrilla warfare tactic.

1) Prepare yourself for the trouble by finding out what's in the note. There are three basic methods for doing this:

   a) Steam it open

b) Hold it up to a strong lightbulb

c) Using binoculars (or a radio-telescope) try to read it over your mum or dad's shoulder.

2) Prepare the ground before you deliver it – for instance:

a) Before handing it over get in your parents' good books – offer to do some washing-up, clean their car, take the dog for a walk – in very extreme cases you could even tidy your room!

3) On your way home accidentally

Drain

Drop
(Accidentally.)

note

drop the note so that it falls down a grating just before the council drain-sucking machine comes and vacuums it up.

FRIEND OR FOE

Please don't think that survival at school just means coping with, or getting the better of teachers, silly rules, punishments, lollipop men and women, homework and inedible food.

There's more to it than that. School may be a jungle – but there are other people in the jungle (not just wild, rabid animals like school secretaries). There are OTHER CHILDREN. (As the old saying goes 'No child is an island'.)

Making friends with the RIGHT OTHER CHILDREN, and avoiding making enemies of the WRONG OTHER CHILDREN, is a survival skill of the utmost importance. Get in with the wrong gang and you're done for.

In this fascinating section we show you how, using your classmates' star signs, you can correctly read their characters and thus win the right friends and avoid making deadly enemies.

Simply find out when their birthdays are then use the following unique Survival Guide Horoscope Chart to see if they would be useful friends, or dangerous enemies!

THE SCHOOL SURVIVAL GUIDE'S SPECIAL SCHOOLKIDS' HOROSCOPE CHART

ARIES March 21–May 21

These kids think they are rams (actually kids are goats — get it?). Anyway, they're inclined to be bossy and they butt in all the time and tell you what to do. Best avoid them.

TAURUS April 22–May 21
They're a bit like Aries Rams, except that they think they are bulls. They butt in all the time and tell you what to do – best avoid them (especially if you live in a china shop).

GEMINI May 22–June 22
They are inclined to be twins. No one knows why this is. Gemini is what's called an 'air sign' so these people are inclined to be airy fairy air-heads, who can't concentrate for two minutes on anything.

19

CANCER June 23–July 23
Cancer is the sign
of the crab, so
people born under
this sign walk
sideways. They
therefore make
rotten friends,
because if you try to

walk to school with one of them they
keep pushing you in the ditch (or
nipping you with their savage
pincers).

LEO July 24–August 24
They are rather like
rams and bulls
(see Aries and Taurus,
above) except
that they think
they're lions. They
stalk around the
place acting like
Kings of the Jungle.
Terrible big-
heads. Keep well
away from them.

VIRGO August 24—September 23

Frightful old fusspots. They've got tidy bedrooms — can you believe it!? They wear aprons and dust things! They fiddle-faddle around with tiny details that no one else in their right mind would care two hoots about.

LIBRA September 24—October 23

Librans think they are kitchen scales. This means that they are very keen on 'balance' and being fair. If you've got five sweets and you give a Libran one they say: 'Hey! That's not fair! It's not balanced. I want two and a half sweets exactly!' Enough said?

SCORPIO October 24—November 22
They're scorpions — deadly dangerous and not to be trusted. They may seem nice enough in a creepy-crawly sort of way — but beware: there's inclined to be a sting in the tail.

SAGITTARIUS November 23— December 21

Sagittarians are really odd. They are half horses and half archer. This means apparently that about half of them like horses — and the other half like archery. They are also supposed to be very wise and into freedom — so what?

CAPRICORNS December 22–January 20

These kids really are goats! (Only kidding! – get it?) They are slow and stubborn, with horns, and they're very mean with money. This fact alone means that they are hopeless as friends.

AQUARIUS January 21–February 19

Aquarius is the sign of the water-carrier. They make surprisingly good friends, but only if you need a lot of water carrying somewhere. If you don't you'll probably find them to be rather wet, soppy creatures.

PISCES February 20–March 20

Pisceans behave like fish — usually goldfish, so if you see a kid in the playground walking round in circles and blowing imaginary bubbles out of its mouth, that's a Piscean. Avoid them — they're totally nuts.

GLORIA SLOPBUCKET'S PROBLEM PAGE

SURVIVAL TIPS *FROM OUR VERY OWN AGONY AUNT*

Got a problem? Worried, anxious terrified? Write to kind old 'Auntie' Gloria Slopbucket; her no-nonsense answers will set your mind at rest. (As Gloria herself often says: 'A problem shared is a problem doubled!'*)

Dear Auntie Gloria,
My hobby is football, but next term I thought I'd start going to ballet lessons. But I'm worried; will the lads in the football team tease me?
Yours sincerely,
Robert 'Wimpo' Wibble

Dear Robert, Yes.

*She sometimes also says: 'What's the point of living if you can't listen to other people's misfortunes and have a good laugh at them?!'

Dear Gloria,
I'm worried. This week it was my turn to feed our school cat. I went down to the supermarket and bought a lovely big bag of cat litter, but it hasn't eaten any of it. What is wrong?
Yours   Jemima Tinkleberry

Dear Jemima, Look, you idiot — cats don't eat cat litter — they sort of sit on it. Don't you know anything? Cat litter is a kind of granular blotting paper used in cats' lavatories. (Incidentally, it's also very handy for soaking up those unsightly puddles of blood and stuff that you sometimes get after playground fights, school riots, mixed ping-pong matches, etc.) Buy the poor little creature some Mice Crispies before it flakes out!

Dear Gloria,
I think I'm turning into a pair of curtains.
Yours,
    Honeylegs McGinty

Dear Honeylegs (what a stupid name), Pull yourself together ...

Dear Auntie Gloria,
Everytime I drink a mug of school tea I get this terrible stabbing sensation up my nose. Is there something wrong with me?
Yours etc,
Jeremy Ganderhead-Smythe

Dear Jeremy, Try taking the spoon out of the mug before you start drinking. Twit!

Dear Auntie Gloria,
The children at school call me 'sissy' and 'girl's blouse' and 'goody-goody' and 'whoopsy-knickers'. What should I do?
Jim Grunge,

Dear Jim, Slosh them with your handbag of course.

Dear Ms. Slopbucket,
I like doing ballet, but next Saturday I've been invited to play rugby league as a front row forward for Rochdale Hornets against Hull Kingston Rovers. I'd like to play - but if I do will the girls at ballet class tease me?
Yours,
Griselda Gump

Dear Griselda, Not if they've got any sense they won't.

A FIELD GUIDE

TO COMMON SPECIES
OF TEACHER

Survival in the wild depends on being able to spot dangerous species. Here's vital information to help you to identify some common staff-room specimens found in modern, or not so modern, schools . . .

OLD CODGERS

LATIN NAME: *Tutorus Claptoutus*

COMMON NAMES: Reg, Stanley, Eric, Ted, Arthur, Frank

APPEARANCE AND PLUMAGE

OLD CODGERS are male, and frequently bald. They usually wear sports jackets, often brown or green, and with leather patches on the elbows and round the cuffs.

Red or blue ballpoint pens are frequently to be spotted in their top pockets, with tell-tale ink splodges on their upper body and hands. Their trousers are always old, with turn-ups and grey handkerchiefs in the pockets. The less you think about their socks and underwear the better.

OLD CODGERS' shoes are usually brown leather, with worn heels. Extreme cases sometimes use string for shoelaces, and can be seen in wet weather running with a strange, high-stepping hop through puddles; this is probably because their shoes leak.

Beware: the more dangerous specimens often have revolting moustaches.

29

DISTINGUISHING CHARACTERISTICS

Many OLD CODGERS smoke heavily – sometimes pipes – and their cars are a complete mess. Some suck mints. They are inclined to carry old books under their arms. They usually arrive in school just before the bell goes, and leave the moment lessons are over. As they get older they go to the toilet a lot. When teaching they sound as if they've done the lesson hundreds of times before. They have.

SPECIAL WARNING: These teachers often smell a bit like something unpleasant that's been left under the floorboards in an attic for about 300 years.

HAUNTS

OLD CODGERS sit in the oldest chairs in the staff room – nearest the electric fire in winter. They are *never* found on games fields.

Their most natural habitat is actually their nearest pub, greenhouse, or bowling green.

COMMON CALLS

The OLD CODGERS' favourite calls are: 'What on earth's a Nintendo?' 'Only two more years to go!' 'In my day . . .' 'When I was a lad . . .' 'I didn't fight in the war so you could chew gum in my class.' 'Newfangled rubbish!'

JOLLY HOCKEYSTICKS

LATIN NAME: *Anna Bolicus (cum Adidas)*

COMMON NAMES: Jen, Sal, Trish, Liz, Carol, Pat, Sue

APPEARANCE AND PLUMAGE
JOLLY HOCKEYSTICKS are female, and look healthy (they don't look very nice, but they look healthy). Their faces are rather red, and their hair is either short, or tied at the back in a pony-tail. Their legs, often large, are also inclined to be red in colour, with well-scarred knees. JOLLY HOCKEYSTICKS wear whistles tied round their necks on stout pieces of ribbon. Unfortunately they frequently wear track suits, or worse, shell suits.

DISTINGUISHING CHARACTERISTICS

These teachers are usually quite young, and they're crazy about games. They never seem to take any notice of the weather, and can turn very dangerous when crossed by any child who doesn't want to run about in the rain with cold hands and feet wearing silly, inadequate clothing.

HAUNTS

JOLLY HOCKEYSTICKS haunt netball pitches, tennis courts, swimming pools, hockey fields. If found in classrooms they are usually teaching geography.

COMMON CALLS

JOLLY HOCKEYSTICKS blow whistles a lot to attract attention, but they also have some common calls such as: 'Get up, it's not even broken.' 'Run, girl, run!' 'Last one through the ice gets a detention.' 'It's good for you!'

ATTILA THE HEN
LATIN NAME:
Nazi Dragonatum

COMMON NAMES: Eva, Griselda, Ada, Hilda, Gloria, Hannibal

APPEARANCE AND PLUMAGE
ATTILA THE HENS are the least attractive of all staff-room species. In fact they're terrifying. Huge, lumber-

ing females, with hair like wire wool and chins like the bows of battleships. Tweed skirts topped by horrible brown cardigans are common; army boots are not unknown on the most unpleasant specimens. Food stains down their fronts are commonplace, as are warts with white whiskers growing out of the middle of them. (As it would be 'fatist' to point it out, I won't mention that ATTILAS are nearly always fat.)

DISTINGUISHING CHARACTERISTICS

They are one of the very few breeds of teacher who still carry handbags – these are used to hold their handcuffs, ball and chains, and medieval maces with spikes on them. A common feature of ATTILA THE HEN behaviour is that just when you think everything is going well – you've settled down for a nice game of cards behind the bike sheds for instance – when up rushes one of them like a rhino, muttering dark oaths and curses, and spreading misery.

HAUNTS

They can often be heard crashing through playground undergrowth, but this is one of the problems with ATTILAS, they don't stick to their own haunt – which should of course be the staff room – they roam widely, and always when you're not expecting it. (See Distinguishing Characteristics, above.)

COMMON CALLS

GGGRRRRAAAAAARRRR!!!!! or 'Vee

haff ways of making you not talk!'

Special note and survival tip: There is a rare species of ATTILA THE HEN that teaches in convent or Roman Catholic schools – it is called ATTILA THE NUN. **AVOID THEM IF AT ALL POSSIBLE.**

MISS MUFFETS

LATIN NAME: *Spinster Laura Ashlii (vegetariana)*

COMMON NAMES: Jenni, Emma, Daisy, Jilly, Poppy, Susie, Penny

APPEARANCE AND PLUMAGE
In summer MISS MUFFETS wear long frocks with flowers on them. Their winter plumage often includes fluffy woolly jumpers. They have long hair, and are prone to have very fair skin and freckles. You can usually see their toes through their sandals. They often wear embarrassing hats made of straw. They carry things around in wicker shopping baskets, especially rolled-up sheets of coloured sugar paper.

DISTINGUISHING CHARACTERISTICS

At home they often have cats with names like Tibby, and they frequently come to school by bicycle – with a 'Nuclear Power? No Thanks' sticker on the mudguard. MISS MUFFETS are very kind and gentle by nature (they hardly ever shout) but when upset they sob into little white handkerchiefs. They always stay late after school – doing things with the coloured sugar paper. They can frequently play the piano, and do so in Assembly.

HAUNTS

MUFFETS have only one haunt – the Infants' Classrooms.

COMMON CALLS

The calls are uttered in soft tones – among the most common being: 'I don't think that's very sensible, do you?' 'Now, have we all washed our hands?' 'Time to clear away.' 'What a lovely picture! Well done!'

(See page 43 for Beatrix Potty Schools)

HI, GUYS!
LATIN NAME: *Oneofus Familiarus*

COMMON NAMES: Dave, Mick, Barry, Terry, Jim, Steve
APPEARANCE AND PLUMAGE
HI, GUYS! are a common species of young male teacher. They are harmless, and indeed, very friendly. Their general aim in life is to be 'One of us', and to break down the differences between pupils and teachers in schools.
They often wear jeans and singlets, or jumpers with patterns on. Extreme cases wear tops with writing on –

things like 'The Pet Shop Boys are Really Great!' 'Save the Whale, Guys, OK?' Really advanced cases may be seen wearing a sweatshirt with the name of the school they teach at on it! Sometimes they have wispy beards – a bit like the fur in a poodle's armpit. They never wear ties.

DISTINGUISHING BEHAVIOUR

The easiest way to tell if you've got a HI, GUYS! teacher is to listen to what they say. COMMON CALLS are therefore important. These include the use of words like 'guys' 'folks' 'right on, lads and lasses' (sometimes pronounced 'laddesses' as a really good groovy joke!).

They also say 'OK' a lot, OK?

A typical HI, GUYS! will start a lesson like this:

'Hi, guys! Let's settle down a bit, OK? Now, folks, let's get started. LOOK! Settle down, OK – we're all here to do some work, and that includes me as well as you – life's about sharing, OK?

I wouldn't ask you to do anything I wouldn't do, OK? Now, let's draw lots for who gets to use the tambourine today . . .'

AND FINALLY . . .

SOMETHING ELSIES
LATIN NAME: *Abscondum Miseratum*

A special note is needed here about SOMETHING ELSIES. They are the teachers who can frequently be heard mumbling, *'Actually I didn't want to be a teacher: I could have been SOMETHING ELSE.'*

These teachers are very common, and are impossible to spot until you hear them say this phrase (they usually also look pretty miserable).

Variations on their basic call are often heard. They include things like:

I COULD HAVE BEEN:

A MILLIONAIRE

A SUCCESS

RICH AND FAMOUS

Or

'I might go on the stage one day' . . . 'I won't be here after Christmas' . . . 'I've had it up to here with teaching' . . . 'My brother's a high court judge, you know' . . . 'If I could leave the profession you wouldn't see me for dust' . . . 'I wonder how much the police get paid?' . . . 'or traffic wardens?' . . . 'I'm thinking of going to Australia' . . . 'I WANT TO BE **SOMETHING ELSE!!**'

A USER'S GUIDE TO SCHOOLS

PART TWO:
BEATRIX POTTY'S MIXED INFANT SCHOOLS

Beatrix Potty Mixed Infant Schools are among the sweetest, kindest, cosiest schools in the Kingdom. Usually found in the country, they are particularly suitable for children with names like Peter, Jemima, Benjamin, Jeremy, and Flopsy and Cottontail. (Flopsy and Cottontail?!)

MAIN CHARACTERISTICS
Most good Infant Schools have an element of Beatrix Potty in them. The entrance of a true Beatrix Potty School always has roses growing round it, and the playground often includes a duckpond, some woodland and a sweet little BRAMBLY HEDGE. Inside, all the classrooms have Welsh dressers – as well as nice little chairs, desks and tables.

TEACHING METHODS
The staff consist almost entirely of Miss Muffets and so there's lots of activity involving coloured paper, old yoghurt pots and scissors with round ends that are totally blunt.

There's absolutely masses of Nature Study, Art and Storytelling. As with most types of Infant School there are no real 'lessons' – the children work happily and informally together, at the sand table, in the playground, drawing with fat wax crayons, and – at Beatrix Potty Schools – getting stuck inside watering cans, catching the buttons of

their jackets in strawberry netting, biting each other's tails off, etc.

Games consist almost entirely of playing old-fashioned things like Ninepins and Hunt the Thimble.

UNIFORM?
YES – obtainable from Laura Ashley

FOOD
Mainly nuts and berries, sometimes a little bit of bread and no cheese.

SPECIAL PUNISHMENTS
There are very few punishments at

Potty Schools. The main ones are getting your tail bitten off (see above) or having your nuts confiscated.

GOOD FOR
Very good for Beatrix potty training, and for learning early basic skills like how to draw the underneath of mushrooms very well. Children who like embroidery, kitchen gardening, ballet, fishing, country cooking and drawing the underneaths of mushrooms very well, are likely to thrive at Beatrix Potty Mixed Infant Schools.

BAD FOR
Beatrix Potty Mixed Infant Schools are *not* recommended for children who like ripping the heads off stuffed rabbits, eating frogs' legs with garlic butter, or playing rough games like Rugby Football, British Bulldog or Tax Wrestling.

SCHOOL SURVIVAL ALPHABET

A simple ABC full of definitions and general knowledge essential for survival at school today.

A = ANSWERING BACK: saying anything to a teacher that's cleverer than anything a teacher has just said to you.

B = BURSAR: some schools have people called Bursars who look after the school's money – they can more accurately therefore be referred to as 'Burglars'

C = CROSS-EYED: teachers who are cross-eyed are particularly hopeless – they can't control their pupils.

D = DUCK: the only animal seen at a game of school cricket, except of course bats.

E = EASY EXAMS: sorry, there's no such thing.

F = FOG: something grey and thick – yes, yes, a bit like an old teacher.

G = GROAN-UPS: anyone who moans a lot, for example an adult.

H = HELL: something that going to school teaches you to believe in.

I = IG: an Eskimo's house with no toilet.

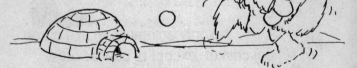

J = JANITOR: a sort of odd-job man found in some schools – generally they have moustaches and are unpleasant.

K = KNIGHT: a medieval soldier who went to knight school.

L = LEMMING: hopeless and rare classroom pets which keep diving off desks and tables.

M = MULTI-PLIERS: tools used in arithmetic.

N = NEEDLEWORK: school subject taught by teachers who are right old sew-and-sews.

O = OCTOPUS: a dangerous, well-armed sea creature.

P = POCKET CALCULATORS: useful instruments which tell you how many pockets you've got.

Q = QUESTION MARKS: what school tests are all about – questions, and marks.

R = REGISTER: a list of prisoners.

S = SCHOOL SWAT: clever little kid you pick up and kill flies with.

T = TUNA: a musical fish – PIANO TUNAS sometimes visit schools.

U = UNMUSICAL INSTRUMENT: see Violin, below.

V = VIOLIN: instrument of torture.

W = WOODWORK: school lesson where it's important not to bite your nails.

X = XYLOPHONE: see Unmusical Instrument, above.

Y = YAWN: expression of enthusiasm in Scripture or RE class; it shows you're still awake.

Z = ZERO: easiest number to score in any school test.

BY THE WAY...

IF YOU'RE ONE OF THOSE PEOPLE WHO LOOKS THROUGH BOOKS IN BOOKSHOPS WITHOUT BUYING THEM, AND YOU'VE GOT THIS FAR IN THIS ONE — WE'D JUST LIKE TO POINT OUT THAT WE'RE WATCHING YOU.

WE SUGGEST THAT YOU EITHER COUGH UP THE SMALL AMOUNT OF POCKET MONEY THAT IT'LL TAKE TO BUY IT, OR YOU PUT IT BACK FOR SOMEBODY ELSE TO BUY. WE NEED THE MONEY.

IF HOWEVER YOU THINK YOU'D PREFER TO LOOK THROUGH SOME OF ROALD DAHL'S BOOKS THEY'RE JUST BEHIND YOU ON THE LEFT, ABOUT HALF WAY DOWN THE SHELVES

THANK YOU

BROUGH GIRLING
        AND
    JUDY BROWN

HEADTEACHERS

FROM THE
DAYS OF THE DINOSAUR

MOST headteachers come from the days of the dinosaur. Here we look at four distinct types of Prehistoric Headteacher — it's highly likely that your headteacher is one of these, but check page 76 in case you've got a modern specimen.

WARNING: Modern specimens are just as horrific.

THE WOOLLY MAMMOTH HEAD-TEACHER*

* OK OK, I know woolly mammoths weren't dinosaurs, they were early mammals, but I can't get everything right. Stop being so fussy!

GENERAL REMARKS

WOOLLY MAMMOTHS are nearly always males, and can therefore be more correctly referred to as WOOLLY MAMMOTH HEADMASTERS. Their distinguishing features are obvious. They have large, scruffy beards, which are usually brown or even a very unattractive ginger colour. These beards are sometimes streaked with grey or nicotine yellow – and frequently contain bits of old food – breadcrumbs, egg, bacon rind, cheese all being quite common. Fossilised specimens have even been known to have old cigarette ends hidden deep within their beard and chest hair.

As their name implies, WOOLLY MAMMOTH HEADMASTERS are large, lumbering creatures, with ill-fitting clothes. These nearly always include baggy old sports jackets and terrible trousers – sometimes corduroy. The teeth on a WOOLLY MAMMOTH are large and yellow (but should not to be confused with the SABRE–

TOOTHED HEADTEACHER – see below).

In very extreme cases, hot weather can affect WOOLLY MAMMOTHS badly, causing them to shed their normal stout shoes for really ghastly sandals which they wear with brown or green socks (yuk).

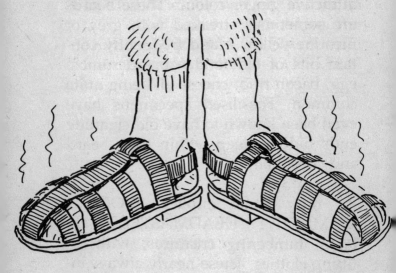

SPECIAL NOTE: Strangely, although WOOLLY MAMMOTH HEAD-MASTERS have hairy faces – and one presumes, hairy legs, arms, bellies, etc. – they are frequently bald on the tops of their heads. It's widely thought that they purposely grow their beards in order to compensate for this fact.

SURVIVAL TIP *Don't ever say to a* **WOOLLY MAMMOTH HEADMASTER: *'Excuse me, Mr —, do you grow that revolting beard just to make up for the fact that you're as bald as a billiard ball?'*
(See WOOLLY MAMMOTH HEADMASTER Behaviour, below.)

BEHAVIOUR AND OTHER CHARACTERISTICS
Although normally a docile, dozy creature, the WOOLLY MAMMOTH can be dangerous when angry (see SURVIVAL TIP above). They can shout loudly, and when annoyed tend to

sweep though classrooms or playgrounds making fearful roaring sounds – rather like a grisly bear with a bad hangover crashing through a North American forest.

AMAZING TRUE FACT: Heavily bearded **female** *WOOLLY MAMMOTHS have occasionally be sighted in Junior Schools, but are thought to be extremely rare (and horrendously dangerous).*

THE SISTER CELIA CANTH (PRO-NOUNCED *COELIACANTH*)

GENERAL REMARKS

It was once thought that SISTER CELIA CANTHS were totally extinct – but a specimen was found in the 1950s and they are now thought to be distributed quite widely in various convent schools.

They are certainly strange, pre-historic looking creatures, with pale white faces and black or grey clothes. A distinguishing feature is their quite incredibly sensible, unfashionable shoes, always black.

Also, they never wear lipstick or other make-up, and if they wear glasses (they often do) they are the opposite of the type of glasses worn by Dame Edna Everage. The skin on a Celia Canth is usually wrinkly. They sometimes have whiskers (yuk).

BEHAVIOUR AND OTHER CHARAC-
TERISTICS
Unlike the WOOLLY MAMMOTH HEADMASTER, SISTER CELIA CANTHS hardly ever get angry. They are quite strict, but are gentle and kind as well. Their voices are likewise usu-

OH DEAR ME, HOW AWFULLY PAINFUL!

ally soft. They are probably the only breed of headteacher that never swears, even in private (see page 82).

Smoking by CELIA CANTHS is also extremely rare – especially pipes and cigars.

SPECIAL NOTE: Anyone spotting a SISTER CELIA CANTH smoking a pipe or cigar should notify the British Natural History Museum immediately.

AMAZING TRUE FACT: The following items are NEVER found on SISTER CELIA CANTHS:
Baseball caps
Swatch watches
Doc Martins (especially ones with metal toe caps)
Two-piece swimming costumes
Wrist slap bracelets
Kiss-me-quick hats
Betting slips
Tattoos
T-shirts with 'GEORGE MICHAEL – COME AND GET ME' written on the front.

THE DIPLODOCUS – or 'DIPPY' HEADTEACHER.

As is well known, most dinosaurs had brains the size of a walnut. If you think your headteacher has a brain the size of a walnut, especially a very small walnut, he or she is almost certainly a DIPLODOCUS HEADTEACHER.

Both male and female DIPLODOCUS are common in schools, and are usually called 'Dippies'. You can tell for certain if you've got a Dippy Headteacher because they say incredibly stupid things – especially in Assembly. Things like: 'I want all the children who are going on the school trip tomorrow to be on their best behaviour.' As anyone knows this is a particularly 'dippy' thing to say. *What on earth is the point of going on a school trip if you've got to be on your best behaviour?*

OTHER TOTALLY DIPPY THINGS THEY SAY:

'Put your hand up at the back if you can't hear me.'

'Would you behave like that at home?'

'How would you like it if I did that to you?'

'I'm looking forward to seeing all your parents at the Parents' Evening.'

'I wasn't born yesterday, you know.'

THE SABRE-TOOTHED HEADTEACHER

If you've got a SABRE-TOOTHED HEADTEACHER – bad luck. They are among the most savage, bloodthirsty and vicious types of teacher who still roam free on the Earth.

Their main distinguishing characteristic is the way they prowl around the place, looking for innocent victims to savage. They have, of course, vicious teeth, but then they've got vicious faces and tempers to go with them. When trying to decide whether your headteacher is a SABRE-TOOTH or not, watch out for tell-tale bloodstains down their cardigans.

Typical SABRE-TOOTH behaviour is when, for instance, you're minding your own business – say sitting on a radiator during break, or swapping football stickers, or discussing yesterday's late night TV with your friends, when in they stalk, and with a blood-chilling yell, they shout: 'GET OUT INTO THAT PLAYGROUND BEFORE I TURN YOU INSIDE OUT AND BUTTER YOUR REMAINS ALL OVER THE FOOTBALL PITCH!!'

SURVIVING A NEW TRICK

Watch out! Teachers have got a new trick up their sleeves.

It's called Aural History – and in case you haven't had to do it yet, here's what it is. Teachers tell you to talk to the old members of your family or community about what life was like when they were young (i.e. about a thousand years ago).

You then have to write down what the dear old fossils have told you; and that's the problem. If you write down what they *really* say you'll probably end up with no marks, a detention or two, and a rotten school report!

In this section of your Survival Guide to School we show you how to translate the Aural History you hear into the Aural History your teacher actually wants to read.

FOR INSTANCE:

1. Suppose you ask your gran, 'What was it like in the Second World War, Gran? What did you do?'

Your gran will probably whisper something like this: 'EEEeee, don't tell your Granddad, but we had a high old time! When he went off to the war the village filled up with American soldiers who were stationed at the air base. OOOH, you should have seen them! (I said not to tell your granddad, didn't I?) They were all muscles, Brylcreme and big smiles! And they had chocolates and nylons and whisky and lovely white teeth! Smashing lads they were. We danced the nights away I can tell you! (Don't tell Grandad.)'

For the purposes of Aural History this needs to be translated as follows:

Life in wartime was very tough. We didn't have TV or anything like that, and had to make our own entertainments. I worked in a factory making Spitfire aeroplanes, and had to get up at five o'clock every morning, and we didn't have indoor toilets.

2. If you ask your grandfather, 'Did you have to fight in the Second World War, Granddad?' he'll probably say: 'Well now, I had a bit scrap with a Scotsman once, behind the Dog and Pheasant at Catterick. Don't tell your granma, but we fell out over this smashing young landgirl I'd taken a bit of a shine to!! Lovely pair of ankles she had . . . Anyway, I blacked the blighter's eye for him, which was pretty good going considering I'd had eighteen pints of mild and bitter — I said don't tell your grandmother, didn't I?'

Aural History translation:

The life of a soldier was very hard. But because you knew you were fighting for King and Country you put up with the privations of life in the army. The cheerful companionship of other soldiers was often what kept us going.

Get the idea?

SCHOOL SURVIVAL: ANOTHER

SPECIAL WARNING

IF YOUR TEACHER GROWLS A LOT, WEARS A LEATHER COLLAR ROUND ITS NECK WITH BIG BRASS STUDS ON IT, SPEAKS AND LOOKS A BIT LIKE ARNOLD SWATZENEGGER AND DRIBBLES OR EVEN FROTHS AT THE MOUTH, BEWARE, YOU'VE ALMOST CERTAINLY GOT

AN AMERICAN PIT-BULL TEACHER

SURVIVAL HINTS

If this is the case take the following precautions:

1) Get it registered.
2) Throw it bits of red meat from time to time.
3) Whatever you do – don't annoy it!

4) Call the RSPCA and ask them to come to school and put it down (or alternatively try and shoot it yourself when no one is looking).

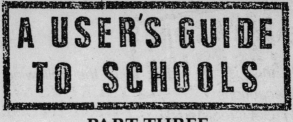

A USER'S GUIDE TO SCHOOLS

PART THREE:
THE BRITISH MUSEUM JUNIOR SCHOOLS

Like the British Museum itself, BRIT-ISH MUSUEM JUNIOR SCHOOLS are full of dusty old fossils – and that's just the teachers!

Because they are museum pieces, these schools are extremely old-fashioned, in fact they are medieval and belong in the Dark Ages.

YOUR PARENTS ALMOST CERTAINLY WENT TO ONE OF THESE SCHOOLS.

MAIN CHARACTERISTICS

The school buildings are of course very old, with bare wooden floorboards and windows like windows out of a church. All BRITISH MUSEUM SCHOOLS have old wooden blackboards, and rows of antique* desks with lids that lift up and small inkwells in the top of them. There are often maps of the British Empire on the walls – but nothing else.

The teachers are nearly all men, usually nicknamed 'Chalky' or 'Wacker Wilkins'. They wear black gowns and carry canes for beating pupils with, and they're aged about 120.

---

* *Antiques are very valuable. Have you thought how much you could get for your parents in an antique shop?*

The girls in these schools are always called either Bunty, Jacky or Jill (in which case they have two ponies). The boys are called Bunter, Jennings, Lord Snooty, Derbyshire, Molesworth or just William.

TEACHING METHODS

The main thing about the teaching in these schools – except for the fact that all the pupils ever do is get caned all day – is that they teach Latin – Latin! No one knows why Latin is taught: it's the only language on earth except double-dutch that nobody speaks.

UNIFORM

Yes, there's lots of uniform. The boys wear caps, blazers and grey shorts. The girls wear something called 'gymslips'. No one knows what they are. The girls' uniform also includes hockey sticks that have to be carried at all times.

FOOD

BRITISH MUSEUM SCHOOL food is the worst food known to man (or schoolchildren). Like most things in these schools the food is known by nicknames, so we need to translate the menu into modern English, for instance:

Dead Man's Leg   Steak and gristle pudding in suet

Rabbit Dropping Pie   Any pudding with currants in it

Snotty Sauce	Custard
Giant's Eyes	Underdone fried eggs
Cow Muck	Mince and gravy
Frogspawn	Tapioca pudding
Worm Stew	Spaghetti
Dead Fly Pies	Eccles cakes
Dog Dirt on a Pillow	Sausages in batter

PUNISHMENTS

Minor offences are always punished with millions of lines. Anything at all serious – like forgetting to say 'please' – is punished by corporal punishment, i.e. getting hit with sticks, canes, whips, gym shoes, slippers, riot policemen's truncheons.

Really naughty pupils are dealt savage blows across the bottom with long-range inter-continental ballistic missiles.

GOOD FOR
Despite the nonsense about Latin, these schools are actually very good at teaching languages – particularly their own language. It consists of strange expressions like: 'I say, you chaps!' 'blooming crikey, fellows!' 'Hey, what a chizz!' 'Last one out of this dorm will have to see Old Wilks before double prep!' 'Lashings of Frogspawn and Snotty Sauce please, Matron, or I'll be hells batey!'

BAD FOR
Learning about anything to do with the twentieth century.

SPECIAL COMMENTS
The fact that your parents probably went to one of these schools explains quite a lot.

MODERN HEADTEACHERS HA!

You have already read about HEAD-TEACHERS FROM THE AGE OF THE DINOSAURS, and we now come to MODERN HEADTEACHERS.

It's a quite extraordinary fact that there is only one type of MODERN HEAD-TEACHER.

The males of the species are called GREY-SUIT-BANK-MANAGER HEADMASTERS, and the females are called GREATER-SHOULDER-PAD HEADMISTRESSES.

Let's look first at the males. As their name suggests they wear grey suits. They carry briefcases full of papers and books with titles like 'How to Run an Opted-Out School' and 'Vicious Tests and Exams for Four Year Olds'. Sometimes they carry clipboards, and they always have pocket calculators in their pockets.

They have very short hair, no beards (unlike Woolly Mammoth Headteachers – see page 52) white shirts – sometimes with fine stripes – and smart ties. In fine weather Grey-Suit-Bank-Manager Headmasters may take off their grey jackets to reveal pale blue shirts with short sleeves and breast pockets full of calculators and red pens. Unlike Woolly Mammoths they never EVER wear sandals – even in heatwaves.

Now, GREATER-SHOULDER-PADS
Greater-Shoulder-Pad Headmistresses are female equivalents of Grey-Suit-Bank-Manager Headmasters. They are

very determined, dynamic headmistresses (the exact opposite of Miss Muffet teachers). Greater-Shoulder-Pads wear red lipstick, and march around their schools being very managerial – which is another word for bossy.

THE THINGS THEY SAY

Modern Headteachers have several common calls, the most frequently heard being:

'But that's not in the National Curriculum!'

'What is the Chess Club's return on capital invested expressed as a percentage of per capita Council Tax after inflation?!'

'This school is a multi-faceted facility dedicated to inter-Community co-reactive care provision.'

No one knows what any of these calls actually mean.

SURVIVE

IN FOREIGN LANGUAGES!

No one can, of course, survive in Foreign Language lessons. If you're being taught French, German, Spanish, Swahili, Russian, Latin or Greek you just have to sit there and do them: bad luck. But there is a useful and important way that you can use foreign languages to help you survive school life.

You can use them as a code – to say things that you don't want other people to understand.

Here are some useful *foreign language phrases* – all perfectly safe to use (so long as the person who hears you say them doesn't speak the language you say them in!). The sentence in italics shows you how to pronounce the phrase.

THE TEACHERS IN THIS SCHOOL ARE ALL OFF THEIR TROLLEYS!
FRENCH: Dans cette école, les professeurs sont tous completement cinglés!

PRONOUNCED: *Don set aicoll lay professer son toos completmon sanglay!*

HEY, GO AND STICK YOUR HEAD IN A BUCKET.
GERMAN: Scher dich zum Teufel!
PRONOUNCED: *Share dich zoom toyfull!*

THIS SCHOOL GETS ON MY WICK!
SPANISH: Este colegio me da cien patadas!
PRONOUNCED: *Estay colegio may de thee-en patadas!*

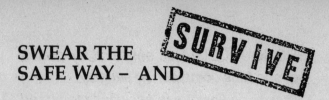

SWEAR THE SAFE WAY – AND SURVIVE

OK, anyone with any sense knows that swearing is a horrible, lousy, loutish thing to do. No one should ever swear.

However, we can hide the truth no longer. We have to tell you that teachers sometimes swear, or, to put it more politely, they use 'expletives'* sometimes.

Here is a list of circumstances under which all known breeds of teacher (except Sister Celia Canths, see page 57) are guaranteed to swear:

1) *When they find a parking ticket on their car.*

* 'Expletives' are swear-words.

2) *When the phone rings early on a Sunday morning, and as they're groping their way downstairs to answer it they tread on a roller-skate that one of their children has left on the top step.*

3) *When they open their monthly bank statement.*

4) *When they come home after a busy night at their local pub or gambling den and discover that the cat has left something very unpleasant in the middle of their living-room floor.*

******!

Swearing, as we've said, is not clever, and this book has no intention of encouraging you to swear in the way teachers do. However, using our special new *School Survival Guide to Safe Swear-words* you should be able to use the odd expletive without committing offence to others, or getting into trouble with your teachers.

Here, for the first time in public, is a new and improved range of carefully graded SAFE SWEAR-WORDS.

MILD:
BELLYBUTTER
NICKERATION
GUSSET
DANGLE
BUMBERNELLERS

STRONG:
FUTTOCK
BELLYBUMBOILS
DUNGHAMMOCK
TWAZZER
GERT BOGWANGLE
FLOB
GUSSARD

EXTRA-STRONG:
DOUBLE-GUSSET!

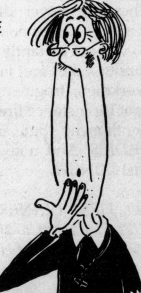

THE SURVIVAL GUIDE

RESPECTING DINNER LADIES

Before we go into the different characteristics of two important breeds of dinner lady, a word is needed about the vital subject of RESPECTING DINNER LADIES.

You will note, for instance, that dinner ladies are always called 'ladies'. They are never dinner 'women'. A 'Lady' is the opposite of 'Gentleman', so you can instantly see how important dinner ladies are. Firemen, policemen, workmen, frogmen, are merely 'men' (not for instance firegentlemen or froggentlemen) but dinner ladies are *LADIES*! And note, it's **DINNER**, not just LUNCH.

SO, FIRST DINNER LADY SURVIVAL TIP: Don't call a dinner lady a 'Lunch Woman' and expect ever to eat again.

NOW: KNOW YOUR DINNER LADIES – AND SURVIVE!

Not many people know that there are, in fact, only TWO breeds of dinner lady, and no one can explain why this should be. However, it's an absolutely vital part of survival at school to be able to tell the two types apart – in fact it's a matter of life and death. (Either slow death by starvation, or sudden death by quick-acting poison.)

The two species are known quite simply as: NICE DINNER LADIES, and NASTY DINNER LADIES.

NICE and NASTY Dinner Ladies look much the same on the outside. (That's one of the tricky things about identifying them.) For instance they dress the same. Their clothing usually consists of large blue dresses with flowers on, but these are frequently covered by aprons or even house-coats, which ban be white or coloured. All dinner ladies work with their sleeves rolled up.

The shoes are always of the comfortable variety; sand shoes, gym shoes, and plimsoles are common, but look out for worn-out examples of rare, early types of trainer. Bedroom slippers are not unknown.

In some schools small caps or hats are worn, generally cow-pat shaped but in off-white or a fetching shade of grey.

By the way: nearly all dinner ladies have large bosoms.

SECOND DINNER LADY **SURVIVAL TIP** *Don't remark on the largeness of a dinner lady's bosom if there's any chance that she can hear you.*

The difference between NICE and NASTY dinner ladies can only be seen in their facial characteristics, and how they behave:

NICE DINNER LADIES
For a start they smile, sing and whistle while they work. Nice dinner ladies like food, and they like schoolchildren, and they like putting the two together.

When ladling custard, jam, gravy, Bolog' sauce or semolina pudding on to your plate they are inclined to be generous (much too generous if it's semolina pudding). They ask you if you'd like some more.

If there is a huge, unidentified lump in your custard, an old sticking plaster in your salad, black bits in your mashed potato or fag ends in your stew, they'll take your plate back without making a fuss about it. They understand that chips are important to you, and that to most children lettuce and tomato and cucumber are a complete waste of a dinner break.

In short – nice dinner ladies are the dinner ladies who seem to be on your side.

They travel to and from school on large buses.

NASTY DINNER LADIES

Nasty dinner ladies *never* smile. They are miserable old cows and you often wonder why they come to work in school at all.

They often have warts on their faces and horrible moustaches. Their necks have boils on the back of them and the skin on their arms and hands looks like corned beef. We mustn't talk about their legs because that would be sexist (and might make us feel a bit sick).

They are stingy with food, especially good stuff like burgers and chips. If you ask for a bit more (or a bit less) of anything, they growl at you.

They travel to and from school on large broomsticks.

SERIOUS ILLNESSES
HOW TO FAKE THEM!

The ability to fake serious illness is a very useful school survival skill. You can use it to get out of exams, tests, plays, punishments, having to read a poem in Assembly, etc, etc.

IT'S SIMPLE! Here's what you do:
1) Fill a hot water bottle and put it in your bed.
2) Get a piece of raw fish from the fridge.
3) Dust your face with flour to make it very pale.
4) Get hold of one of your mum's red lipsticks.
5) Draw red spots all over your face.
6) Eat a yellow boiled sweet.
7) Get into your bed.
8) Look miserable.
9) Call your mum or dad, in a weedy little voice: 'Please . . . I don't feel very well . . .'

When your mum or dad come into your bedroom they'll be horrified to

see how ill you look (white face, red spots, yellow tongue) and they'll go and get the thermometer.

When they start to take your temperature, ask them for a glass of water. When they're out of the room take the thermometer out of your mouth and put it on the hot water bottle.

When they discover that your temperature is only just off the boil your parents will have a fit!! When they try to hold your hand under the bedclothes make sure they grab the piece of raw fish.

WITH A BIT OF LUCK THEY'LL KEEP YOU AT HOME FOR A WEEK!!

BEING IN THE
NATIVITY PLAY

Your chances of surviving being in the School Nativity Play depend entirely on which part you've got in it.

The first and most important thing to understand about the Nativity Play is that no one gets to play the Baby Jesus. This is because the Baby Jesus is always just a doll brought in specially by one of the girls in the year below yours.* This is a pity, because being Baby Jesus would be quite easy, and non-hazardous: you'd just have to lie there, in swaddling clothes, being new-born and receiving rather strange presents.

* SPECIAL SURVIVAL TIP *You can bring the play to an early conclusion if the doll is a Tiny Tears or bed-wetting doll. Simply fill it to the brim with water, and*

hope for the best. But see below for a more reliable way to stop a Nativity Play.

The MOST hazardous parts in the Nativity Play are Mary and Joseph.

NATIVITY PLAY SURVIVAL TIP
Unless you're a total show-off, and therefore a complete pain to have around the house, don't get selected to play Mary or Joseph. If you're at an all-boys school, not being Mary is particularly important: *you'll be teased for a year.*

(If, despite trying really hard not to, you get selected for either of these parts – see our *Special Mary and Joseph Nativity Play Survival Tactic* below.)

Being one of The Three Kings is not as danger-free as you might think. Not only do you have to manage to say words like: 'Let us go forth even unto Bethlehem to see this thing which hath come to pass,' but when you kneel in front of the crib to give your gift, one of the other Three Kings will almost certainly be standing on the edge of your cloak.

This can happen with Shepherds' blankets too, but they do less kneeling, and say less words than the Kings, so are safer parts to play. There are also more of them so it's easier to get lost in the crowd. (It's also sometimes possible to hide behind a cardboard sheep for much of the play.)

Being an Angel is tricky – I mean for a start do you LOOK like an Angel? And their wings often fall off.

Being a cardboard sheep, camel, or shining star is probably the best way to survive the Nativity Play Experience.

SPECIAL MARY AND JOSEPH NATIVITY PLAY SURVIVAL TACTIC
If you are Mary or Joseph, and you want to shorten the whole play and get home as soon as possible, there is

a survival tactic which works every time.

Be very nice to the child playing The Inn Keeper – you may have to bribe him but as you'll see the Three Kings and a few Shepherds will probably chip in – and get him to alter his lines.

When he is supposed to say to you:
'I'm sorry, for there's no room at the inn.'
get him to say instead:
'No problem, Squire! I've got a very nice twin room on the front – with a cot, hot and cold water, colour TV and tea-making facilities!'

This will almost certainly bring the play to an abrupt halt.

A USER'S GUIDE TO SCHOOLS

PART FOUR: ST DRACULAR'S PREPARATORY SCHOOLS

These awful schools are more properly called ST DRACULAR'S PREPARATORY SCHOOLS FOR THE SONS AND DAUGHTERS OF GENTLEFOLK.

MAIN CHARACTERISTICS
Commonly known as St Dracs, they are usually built on rocky promontories or outcrops, in wilder parts of the

country. They always have twisty stairs leading to high pointed turrets with spikey roofs. The weather at St Dracular's is often particularly poor, with black cloud-filled skies swirling above them, and forks of lightning piercing the lashing rain. Large black crows or ravens circle the pointed turrets. The doors always creak – especially the large black wooden front door with its huge heavy black metal knocker.

One other thing: the welcome when you arrive at one of these schools is surprisingly civil. A large and ancient butler (who's often had a bit of facial plastic surgery) will say something like: 'Welcome – Master was expecting you . . . Ha Ha Ha Ha!'

TEACHING METHODS

These are usually traditional, and ignore the National Curriculum. If you can't remember something, your memory is jogged with the use of thumbscrews, hanging you upside-down from metal rings in the wall, or stretching you out on large wooden racks. All this may seem very medieval. It is, but interestingly more modern scientific methods are also used, especially inserting large bolts through pupils' necks, and wiring their bodies up to large machines with levers and loads of high voltage electricity.

FOOD

There's not much food at St Dracular's Preparatory Schools, though pupils are sometimes given strange things to drink by mad-looking science teachers in white coats. These drinks come from large test tubes, and always have green or orange smoky stream coming off the top of them.

SPECIAL SURVIVAL TIP *If you go to a St Dracular's Preparatory School and your tomato soup starts to congeal – don't drink it!*

COMMON PUNISHMENTS
The torture chamber of St Dracs is seldom out of use! Detentions usually last up to five years, and are done hanging upside-down from chains, or in rather uncomfortable metal cages, suspended from the upper battlements.

GOOD FOR

St Dracular's encourage few outdoor sports – but learning how to cross-country run across misty moors pursued by packs of slavering dogs longing to tear your throat out is definitely one of them!

Nature Study is also usually confined to study bats, large black birds (see Crows and Ravens above), hairy black spiders and poisonous snakes. History and geography concentrate on the study of Transylvania.

NOTE: St Dracular's can be particularly good for highly strung children: it highly strings them from the roof.

BAD FOR

Perhaps because they are always built on rocky promontories, in thick woods and remote areas, playing field facilities are poor. No one for instance, ever plays cricket, rounders or softball at these schools. St Dracular's are not generally thought suitable for children who are vegetarians, or wet the bed, or for young people who are sensitive about finding two small unsightly holes in their necks in the middle of the night.

SPECIAL COMMENTS

If you go to a St Dracular's – bad luck (you may feel better when you wake up).

THAT'S NO EXCUSE

NEW, IMPROVED REASONS FOR NOT
HANDING IN HOMEWORK

As you'll probably know by now, if you
haven't done your homework and you give
your teacher one of the three standard
excuses:

1. 'I forgot my book.'
2. 'My mum said we had to visit our nan.'
3. 'My pencil broke.'

it doesn't get you anywhere. Teachers just
roll their eyes and say: 'That's no excuse!'

Good excuses need to have three distinct
qualities: S-URPRISE, O-RIGINALITY and
B-ELIEVABILITY – in other words a SOB
Rating.

Before using a School Survival Guide's NEW, IMPROVED excuse for not handing in your homework, test it first by working out its SOB Rating. Here's an example.

'Please Mr/Miss/Mrs (insert your teacher's name . . .), I did my homework, but when I left the house this morning the ink was still wet, so I held it up in the air to dry it, and a golden eagle swooped down and snatched it and carried it off to its nest on a rocky promontory and fed it to its hungry chicks.'

SURPRISE: Out of 10, how Surprised do you think your teacher will be by this excuse? Write your answer here ____

ORIGINALITY: How Original do you think this excuse is – will a teacher have heard it before? Answer here ____

BELIEVABILITY: Will your teacher Believe this excuse? ____

We gave this excuse 9 for Surprise, 7 for Originality, and only 3 for Believability, giving a total SOB rating of 19 out of 30.

That's not bad – any excuse that scores more than 15 is usually worth a try.

Here are some other new, improved Survival Guide Excuses for you to score: try the ones that you score highest on your teacher next time you haven't done your homework . . .

1) Please (insert teacher's name), I did my homework, but when I was passing the newsagent on the way to school a man with a mask ran out of the shop holding a gun and a bag full of the newsagent's money. He shot a passing policeman who fell to the ground bleeding heavily from a wound in the leg. I phoned the ambulance and when it came the ambulance man said, 'Have you got a school exercise book on you?' and I said, 'yes,' and gave him the book with my homework in it. He said that being both firm and absorbent it would make an ideal splint for the wounded policeman's leg and would soon stanch the heavy flow of blood. So my exercise book is now in the hospital, very bloodstained – that's why I can't hand it in.

S___, O___, B___

2) Please (teacher's name), I did my homework but when I left home this morning I took it out of my school bag to check it through one last time and it got caught on the tip of the tusk of a passing rogue elephant who had just escaped from the zoo. The elephant charged across a railway line and then plunged down a deep ravine that opened up when it trod on a disused mine shaft. The RSPCA say if they find the homework they'll deliver it to my house tonight — so I'll bring it tomorrow. OK?

S____, O____, B____

3) Please (teacher's name), I really enjoyed doing my homework last night but I seem to have left it on my desk next to my grandad's magnifying glass. When the sun came up this morning it must have shone through the window and on to the magnifying glass which then caused it to set fire to my book. We called the fire brigade, and they searched the smouldering remains of the whole house, because I told them how important the homework was; but they said they were sorry, they couldn't find it, and anyway it would probably be either burned to a cinder or very wet by now what with all their hoses.'

S____, O____, B____

THE SURVIVAL GUIDE

SCHOOL REPORTS
– AND WHAT THEY
REALLY MEAN . . .!

A lot of school children get very worried about School Reports. They are quite right to – School Reports are very worrying things. Sometimes teachers use them to say horrible things, like:

> Despite strong competition he has managed to maintain his position at the bottom of the class.

But often Reports don't mean exactly what they say. In this invaluable section of your Survival Guide we show you how to translate School Reports into English!

> Adam could be quite good at art if he could control his natural enthusiasm.

What this teacher is really saying is: 'Adam is a complete pain in the art class. He spills the water, splodges paint over other children's pictures, and doesn't listen to word I say (I didn't really want to teach Art anyway, I did it at teacher's training college because I'm no good at Maths and stuff like that).'

> Samantha has had a satisfactory term.

This is the type of report the Head-teacher often writes. What it actually means is: 'Is Samantha Jones the small girl with freckles — or is she that fat kid with the funny specs who never says much?'

Emma will have to work a lot harder in Geography if she is to get satisfactory test marks next term.

This can be translated as: 'Emma is so bad at Geography that it's a miracle to me that she can find her way to school every morning ...'

It has been a pleasure teaching Jeremy this term, and I wish him well for the future.

This means: 'YIPPEEE! I'm leaving this rotten school next week and getting a job on the railways, so as far as I'm concerned Jeremy and his ghastly classmates can go and put their heads down the nearest lavatory!!'

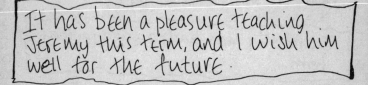

NEWSFLASH! NEWSFLASH!

WE INTERRUPT THIS BOOK
TO BRING YOU AN

IMPORTANT GOVERNMENT HEALTH ANNOUNCEMENT

CONTRARY TO WHAT YOU
MAY HAVE HEARD OR
BELIEVE,
IT IS IMPOSSIBLE TO CATCH

MAD COW DISEASE

FROM DINNER LADIES. *

*(But watch out for SWINE FEVER, FOWL PEST
and FOOT AND MOUTH DISEASE.)

NEWSFLASH! NEWSFLASH!

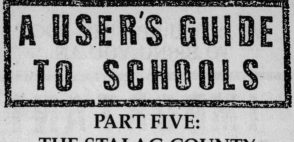

A USER'S GUIDE TO SCHOOLS

PART FIVE:
THE STALAG COUNTY
PRIMARY SCHOOLS

'Stalag' is a foreign word which means, roughly translated, *Prison Camp*. These schools are often quite difficult to get into: they're always almost impossible to get out of.

MAIN CHARACTERISTICS
Look out for barbed-wire entanglements round the boundary inside a high electrified fence, and topped off with watch towers at strategic points such as the corners of the playing fields, and machine-gun posts manned by the teacher on 'playground duty'.

The front gates of Stalag County Primaries are particularly imposing, often comprising sentry posts and red and white barrier poles that go up and down. Parents are never allowed in. (And pupils seldom get out.)

TEACHING METHODS
There's a lot of getting into lines, standing in straight rows, and queuing

up for things. Assembly is held out-doors, whatever the weather. The Register is taken as often as three times a day, to make sure no pupils have escaped during meals or Exercise Break.

UNIFORM?
YES – but it's worn by the staff.

FOOD
The food is often so bad in Stalag County Primaries that the Red Cross or United Nations have to send in food parcels, often dropped from the air by parachute.

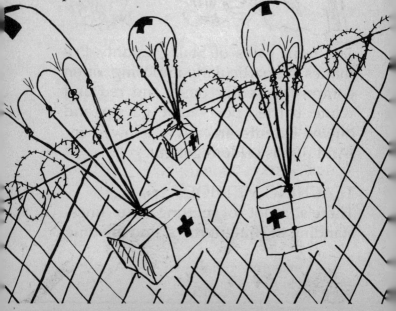

COMMON PUNISHMENTS
Solitary confinement is often used, but small-scale misbehaviour is usually punished by a cuff round the ear with the butt of a rifle. But then going to one of these schools is a bit like doing a very long Detention anyway.

GOOD FOR
Stalag Primary Schools are well known for gym – especially jumping over wooden vaulting horses.

BAD FOR
These schools are generally bad for their pupils.

SPECIAL SURVIVAL TIP *If you are a boarder at one of these schools, don't talk after search lights-out.*

SPECIAL COMMENTS
If you think that you go to one of these schools – *start tunnelling . . .*

SURVIVING PROJECTS

One thing you just can't get out of at school is Projects. Teachers are crazy about them!

As you know, however, teachers are among the most predictable species on Earth, and in the same way that you can always tell what they are going to say (see page 29) you can always tell what projects they are going to give you.

The three main Projects that all teachers are totally crazy on are:
> ROMANS
> VIKINGS
> TUDORS

SURVIVAL NOTE: IT IS IMPOSSIBLE TO GO THROUGH SCHOOL WITHOUT DOING PROJECTS ON ROMANS, VIKINGS AND TUDORS.

So here, to make life easy for you, I give the KEY FACTS you'll need to know in order to survive these three inescapable School Projects.

KEY FACTS ABOUT THE ROMANS:
1. Unlikely as it seems (because they were efficient and highly organised), the Romans were in fact Italians – from Rome, funnily enough.

2. They came to Britain and defeated the Ancient Britons (not surprising, the Ancient Britons were far too old to fight very well – they should have taken on the Fairly Young Britons . . .).

3. History books will tell you that in those days the Ancient Britons dressed

only in blue paint, called 'woad'. I don't think this is right. The fact is that the Ancient Britons had no clothes – and they just looked blue because they were so bloomin' cold. (Few teachers give extra marks if you point this out, but I thought I ought to tell you anyway.)

4. The Romans kept building roads. (All the roads led to Rome.)

5. They also liked building walls. They built one for a guy called Adrian to keep the Scots out. (The Scots came anyway – mainly to play for Leeds and Man United.)

6. The Romans ate meals lying down – try that at school and see where it gets you!

7. The Romans invented the following:
     Central heating bills
     Horrible sandals
     Baths (yuk!)

NOW KEY FACTS ABOUT THE VIKINGS:

1. The Vikings weren't as civilised as the Romans so Projects about them don't usually last so long, and there aren't as many Key Facts.

2. They travelled to Britain in boats which were pointed at both ends. This confused the Ancient Britons – actually it also confused the Vikings – because they didn't know if they were coming or going.

3. The very most important thing about the Vikings is that they had helmets with big horns on the outside (better than helmets with big horns on the INSIDE, eh?).

4. They probably discovered America – but don't tell the Americans that or you'll upset them because they think they were discovered much later by Christopher Columbus. (Actually the North Americans had already discovered America even before the Vikings – but don't tell the Vikings that, you'll upset them too!)

THE TUDORS – KEY FACTS:

1. The Tudors are the world's most popular Project (except maybe the Romans and the Vikings).

2. Queen Elizabeth was the most famous Tudor, then comes Walter Raleigh, inventor of the bike. He also invented other things. For instance he went to America (which had already been discovered by the North American Indians, the Vikings and Christopher Columbus) and invented the potato. This was great because it led to the invention of the chip – and this in turn led to the micro chip on which all modern technology is based!

3. However, when Walter Raleigh tried putting a potato in his pipe he couldn't get it to light, so then he had

to invent tobacco. This was rather a daft thing to do because it makes you cough and is a total waste of money.

4. He put his cloak down in a puddle of mud so that Elizabeth could walk on it. Can you imagine what your mum would say to you if you did that?

'What on earth have you been doing with this cloak??!! It looks as if it's been thrown in a puddle of mud and someone's walked all over it!! No more pocket money for you, my lad! Just wait till your father gets home!!'

5. Another famous Tudor was Francis Drake. He liked ten pin bowling, and defeated something called the Spanish Armadillo, very easily (but don't tell the Spanish or you'll upset them).

SCHOOL SURVIVAL
YET ANOTHER

SPECIAL WARNING

IF YOUR TEACHER HAS SEVERAL ROWS OF INWARD-POINTING TEETH, TOWERS ABOVE YOU AND RIPS CHUNKS OF RED MEAT FROM YOU AND OTHER SMALL MAMMALS, BEWARE, YOU'VE ALMOST CERTAINLY GOT A

TYRANNOSAURUS TEACHER

IF HE'S GOT A DOG, IT'S A **TYRANNOSAURUS REX!**

SURVIVAL HINTS

Unfortunately there's only one way to survive with a Tyrannosaurus teacher. Wait for it to become extinct. (Cheer up, this usually only takes about 30 million years.)

COMPLAINTS

IF YOU HAVE ANY COMPLAINTS ABOUT THIS BOOK THE AUTHOR WOULD LOVE TO HEAR FROM YOU, AS FEEDBACK FROM YOUNG READERS IS EXTREMELY VALUABLE.

HOWEVER, WE WOULD LIKE TO POINT OUT THAT THE LAST PERSON WHO COMPLAINED ABOUT ONE OF THIS AUTHOR'S BOOKS WAS FOUND THREE WEEKS LATER AT THE BOTTOM OF A LAKE WITH LARGE CHUNKS OF CON-CRETE STRAPPED TO THEIR HEAD.

FINAL SURVIVAL TIP

DON'T COMPLAIN ABOUT THIS BOOK.

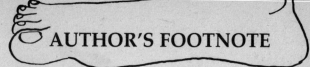

AUTHOR'S FOOTNOTE

I hope you've enjoyed this jokey book about surviving at school: I had a lot of fun writing it!

I also very much hope that you actually enjoy going to school. Most children I meet certainly seem to. However, I do know that for some children surviving at school isn't a joke – I'm thinking particularly of children who suffer from bullying, or from cruel or frightening things that some adults can do to them.

If you are having trouble at school – or at home – and you don't know what to do about it, or who to talk to, you can always phone **CHILDLINE**.

They won't even ask you your name, but they will listen carefully to what you say, and they will certainly be able to help you. The phone call is free, and you can talk as much or as little as you like.

THE NUMBER IS 0800 1111